A GOD-FIRST LIFE

A 21-DAY DEVOTIONAL TO LIVING LIFE GOD'S WAY

Michael & Charla Turner

Turning Point Publishing

ISBN 978-0-578-82525-0

*THIS BOOK IS DEDICATED TO
THE STAFF, LEADERS AND VOLUNTEERS
OF TURNING POINT CHURCH.*

*THANK YOU FOR HELPING US BUILD A HOUSE
THAT IS REACHING OTHERS FAR FROM GOD
WITH THE GOOD NEWS OF JESUS CHRIST,
AND HELPING THEM LEAD A GOD-FIRST LIFE.*

CONTENTS

A God-First Life

CONTENTS

Week 3: GIVING in A God-First Life

Introduction
TODAY MATTERS!

Welcome to a fresh new start! Whether you are reading this devotional at the beginning of a new year, or perhaps a brand new month, it is our prayer that over the next 21 days, you will be able to discover just how you can begin to change what you want this next season in your life to look like. We firmly believe to do so, it starts by making one good choice after the other.

In fact, the choices you and I make daily have lasting results. In other words, today matters!

We all have as human beings certain deep desires and longings. We want to be seen. We want to be known. We want to be loved for who we really are. And all of us, no matter how hard we try to hide it, have a desire to live a purposeful life.

However, many of us are just too busy building up our futures that we forget to build up our lives. The distractions that surround us and fill up our daily routines can cause us to lose sight of the fact that a true life that is fulfilling can only be found in Jesus Christ. A life that is surrendered to Him and puts Him first in everything is what produces the results we want.

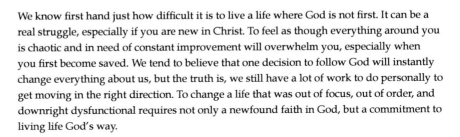

We know first hand just how difficult it is to live a life where God is not first. It can be a real struggle, especially if you are new in Christ. To feel as though everything around you is chaotic and in need of constant improvement will overwhelm you, especially when you first become saved. We tend to believe that one decision to follow God will instantly change everything about us, but the truth is, we still have a lot of work to do personally to get moving in the right direction. To change a life that was out of focus, out of order, and downright dysfunctional requires not only a newfound faith in God, but a commitment to living life God's way.

Introduction

When we were struggling early on in our faith, one of the biggest light bulb moments for us was when our Pastor shared with us what Matthew 6:33 says:

> *But seek first the kingdom of God and his righteousness,*
> *and all these things will be added to you.*

After pouring our hearts and frustrations to him as to why our lives still looked like a mess even after becoming Christians, our Pastor helped us understand that what was missing in our lives was not in fact the presence of God, but order. God's order.

He shared with us that the key to an abundant life was understanding that our God was a God of order, and by prioritizing Him into our lives, it would unlock a major breakthrough for us from that day forward. That all of our issues, all of our wrestling day in and day out to fix our lives would be solved if we just put Him first over all. Well, guess what?

That one Kingdom principle changed our lives forever. To see blessings begin to overflow on us the moment we began to seek God first, we realized that we were finally beginning to live out what our Pastor was trying to show us that day. We were now living a God-first life. And now we want to help come alongside you to do the same. We believe the momentum you are about to create for your life through this 21-day devotion is going to be transformational.

So welcome again to a fresh new start, and welcome to A God-First Life.

Michael & Charla Turne

A FAMILIAR GAME

You will seek me and find me,
when you seek me with all your heart.

Jeremiah 29:13

Day 1: A Familiar Game

When you think of the word "seek" what comes to mind? Perhaps it's that game many of us used to play when we were kids: hide and seek. Before video games and social media took over our lives, a game of hide and seek was all we needed to fill up our day with fun and laughter. For those not familiar with the game, it involved one person or group hiding somewhere, and the other person or group searching to find them.

Some of the kids we used to play this game with hid so well you could never find them. Whereas some didn't hide well, and were always easy to find because of the noise and snickering they would often make. The best part of this game was when after everyone had been found, we would come together and discuss the things that happened during our search. The prize wasn't always being the person who found someone, but the experience we all shared together while seeking.

Do you know that our God wants us to have that same experience with Him? He absolutely loves for us to seek Him daily and desire an intimate relationship with Him.

In fact, God has been seeking a relationship with you from the very start of your life. But it is up to us to also do the seeking. Our God is a perfect gentleman; He never forces us to do anything we don't want to. But He is always inviting us to seek Him and to find Him.

When we seek God, it involves searching for Him and inquiring of Him daily. This is something he wants us to do with all of our heart, our mind, and our emotions. When we seek God with everything we have, we will not only find Him, but we will find the love, wisdom, mercy and grace that we have been missing in our lives. Everything that we've used to fill up the hole in our hearts, our God is perfectly shaped to fill it.

All of us are seeking something in life. Let's make today a day where we seek after God first, knowing that when we find Him, we find life. A life full of pleasure and grace.

EVERYTHING THAT WE'VE USED TO FILL UP THE HOLE IN OUR HEARTS, OUR GOD IS PERFECTLY SHAPED TO FILL IT.

God, thank You for seeking me.
Help me to seek You with all of my heart today.
Show me all the opportunities
to find You in all that I face today.

FIRST THINGS FIRST

*Seek the kingdom of God first
and his righteousness
and all things will be added to us.*

Matthew 6:33

Day 2: First Things First

There is nothing worse than having things out of order in our life. We are unable to function correctly and we are rarely fulfilled as God would want us to be. As Christ followers, we are a part of a beautiful kingdom, whose king has a special way of doing things.

And that way is called righteousness. Whenever we are seeking God first, we are prioritizing His righteousness, His way of doing things over our own. God has an order to all that He has created, and as His creation, the order of our life matters to Him. He wants to know that He always comes first, no matter how busy the day or how urgent the task.

He wants our first.

We cannot afford to let our daily distractions and obligations cause us to miss how important putting Him first truly is. That busyness and desire for instant gratification that we all are tempted to pursue every day, will have us frustrated with the results time and time again. A life without God being first is just like placing a cart before the horse, hoping to see it move.

Nothing good is going to happen from that because what needs to be first is not in place. Remember this: whatever we place in our lives as first we honor. It is something we value as important and critical to our well-being.

When we place God as first in our lives, we are showing Him the honor that He is due. And when we put Him first, we will never be second to anything. Simply because when order is restored, blessing is released. The things we desire from God daily - His presence, His provision, and His promises concerning our lives are released in us and through us when He becomes first.

If you want to see the supernatural happen in your life, and are ready for exponential growth, seek His kingdom first. If you are ready for exponential growth and for your capacity to grow, seek His kingdom first. Worship Him first before anything in your day is added.

Because when you do, He begins to add to your life in a way you never could imagine.

*WHATEVER
WE PLACE
IN OUR
LIVES FIRST
WE HONOR.*

A God-First Life

God, thank You for always guiding me
and helping me follow Your order for my life.
Please help me to identify distractions
and prioritize time with You
before anything or anyone else.
I choose to embrace Your way
of doing things today.

LOVE IN ACTION

*If you love me,
keep my commandments.*
John 14:15

Day 3: Love in Action

It is often said that true love, a love that is authentic and worth pursuing, is one that is unconditional. It requires no prerequisites. And it makes no demands. However, when it comes to demonstrating a love for God, there are in fact a few conditions that exist.

John, the disciple who described himself as the one that Jesus 'loved' above all, said that in order to love God, keeping His commands are essential for us to do. Now we can look at this request as conditional, but either way, it involves us doing something.

It involves action on our part.

As believers, we know that the Word of God contains all of the commands of God. In fact, Jesus is not just found in the Word of God, John describes Jesus as the actual Word of God. When we understand that, we know that the only way to know Him or His commandments is to commit to reading His word daily. Our reading and obeying His word is a sign of worship.

I love what the Passion translation says about what John wrote. It actually says that loving God 'empowers' us to obey His commands. It points to the fact that the more we love God, we have no other option than to obey what He says. When we commit to worshiping Him daily, we discover how worthy He is and how much He deserves our complete devotion.

Our act of worship and obedience to God is not done to make ourselves appear to be worthy in His eyes. Our goal, whether at home, work or at church is to worship in a way where our love for Him is clearly displayed. A worship so pure in spirit that it engages our entire heart.

When we embrace His commandments, we are embracing Him. And when we are keeping His commandments, we are embracing love. Every action of obedience on our part unlocks the love our hearts have been longing for.

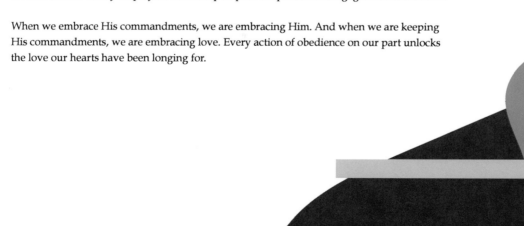

WHEN WE EMBRACE HIS COMMANDMENTS, WE ARE EMBRACING HIM.

God, thank You for loving me.
It is my delight to pour out my love to You.
Help me to embrace obedience today
as my expression of love.

A NEW WHAT IF

"Do not be anxious about anything,
but in every situation, by prayer and petition,
with thanksgiving, present your requests to God.
And the peace of God,
which transcends all understanding,
will guard your hearts
and your minds in Christ Jesus."

Phillipians 4:6-7

A recent study performed by the ADAA, the Anxiety and Depression Association of America, found that an astounding 43% of the population of the United States struggles with worry! In fact, they described it as the most common mental illness in America.

All of us have at one time or another worried about something. No one has ever escaped worry, as it loves to battle for our mind and keep us dwelling on the difficulties of our life. It does everything it can to blind us from solutions and keep us in constant fear. And when we are in fear, we cannot live the abundant and courageous life that God has called us to live.

One of the things I love about observing little children is that they often go about their lives without any fear. Their lack of exposure frees them to imagine what's possible in life, instead of what's negative. I'll never forget playing with my cousins as a small child back in South Carolina. We would love to go to play at nearby lakes, and search for clams in the sand. Whenever we dug them out, we would open them right up. With toes buried in the sand, we would laugh together without a care in the world.

Well let's just say, you couldn't pay me to do that now! As an adult, I now live in the wonderful world of "what ifs." Today, every 'what if' scenario I could think about would make me opt out of going back to that lake. The snake and bug bites. The alligator attacks. Every negative thing I could think of would spark instant worry and fear in me and cause me to only focus on every negative scenario that could happen.

What would it be like to be a child again? To have a childlike faith, free of fear and full of confidence, knowing that we have a wonderful God who loves us and wants to take care of us. Could you imagine a life where you push past every fear, every anxiety and every worry? Well that is the life our God wants us to have. He wants nothing more than to bring more of heaven on earth for us to experience.

Now I know our brains can seem to be hardwired for negativity, but I want you to know that we as believers are able to rewire our brains and develop new positive thoughts and habits. It's not easy, but if we can commit to renewing our mind daily, where we deny ourselves the opportunity to dwell on the negative and focus our attention on a God who is bigger than our problems, everything is possible!

I want to encourage you today to begin to magnify our God. When you magnify God, you are making Him bigger. And the bigger He becomes, the more those "what ifs" begin to disappear and are replaced with a life full of freedom and faith.

WHEN WE ARE
IN FEAR, WE CANNOT
LIVE THE ABUNDANT
AND COURAGEOUS
LIFE THAT GOD HAS
CALLED US TO LIVE.

God, thank You that you are perfecting
all that concerns me and
working all things together for my good.
Your perfect love casts out all fear.
Help me to rest in knowing
that I can trust You every detail of my life.
I receive Your peace today.

FILL IT UP

The disciples were filled with joy and the Holy Spirit.

Acts 13:52

Day 5: Fill It Up

There is nothing quite like having the margin and capacity necessary to enjoy life. When we fill our lives up with doubt, worry, fear and regret, we are left with very little space for God to be worshiped and to dwell with us.

Every single day, we are given the opportunity by God to create space for Him. In fact, did you know that God has given us as believers the authority to decide on what we will fill our hearts with? So many times we find ourselves filling up on distractions and attractions which fill us with envy, discouragement and insecurity. God has given us the ability to choose what we will give our time, energy and focus to. When we choose to worship Him, we are choosing a life full of more of the things we know bring true fulfillment and peace. It is the place where we are most satisfied and God is most glorified!

When you and I choose to worship God in praise, when we confess God's Word over our lives, we are filling ourselves with His Spirit, the Holy Spirit; a spirit of power, love and soundness of mind. As His sons and daughters, we have been given access to His presence, and it is His presence that creates space for us to accomplish all that He has for us. Psalm 16:11 says that in His presence there is fullness us Joy and at his right hand are pleasures forever more. Making room for God is the most important action we can take every day knowing that He will fill me with His Holy Spirit enabling me to live in freedom and victory.

Making space for God means we have to create time for Him. To make room for Him. To acknowledge and focus on Him daily is what will fill our hearts with hope and faith.

When we are willing to empty ourselves and seek Him first above everything else, He is more than willing to fill up our heart with good things. Be filled with the Holy Spirit because He is our teacher, our comforter and helper whenever we are in need.

If you are ready for a day filled with joy, commit to beginning it with worship. Living and leading a God-first life can only be fueled by a heart full of Him. Choose to fill it up today.

MAKING SPACE
FOR GOD MEANS
WE HAVE
TO CREATE TIME
FOR HIM.

God, thank You for always
being available for me.
Help me to always make room for You
in all areas of my life.
You are my priority and
I want to be filled with all that You are.
I can't be filled with You if I'm filled
with the things that are less important.
I choose to live, move and exist in You.

TIME AFTER TIME

Keep this book of the law always on your lips.
Meditate on it day and night
so that you may be careful
to do everything written in it.
Then you will be prosperous and successful.

Joshua 1:8

Day 6: Time After Time

It's been said that the greatest commodity that you and I have in this world is our time. When you think about what we spend most of our time on each day, very little actually brings us the return that we are looking for. It's something that we can never get back if wasted.

However, one of the greatest investments you and I can make with our time is when we commit ourselves to prayer. Not just when we first wake up, but to do so whenever we can, because doing so demonstrates to God that our time with Him is what we value most.

We serve a God that wants us to reflect His nature and image throughout the earth. To reflect His glory to a world so desperately in need of Him. But the only way to do so is to spend time with Him in prayer. You see, it is in prayer that God reveals truth to us. It's where He reveals His treasure. Those secret things that cannot be found in a life that is committed to the world.

No matter how hard we try, Google can't provide what our souls long for each day. Our phones can't provide them either. God is the only source that can provide us with what we need and that is why He is worth our full devotion every opportunity we get.

To devote yourself to something means to meditate on it.

The Word meditate means to have your mind constantly focused on something; to spend time thinking deeply about it without any wavering. When our time with God is one that ceases from wavering, when it is not just an outline for our day, but it becomes the focus for our day, we are able to access a joy and a peace that is truly unshakable.

IT IS IN PRAYER
THAT GOD REVEALS
TRUTH TO US.
IT'S WHERE
HE REVEALS
HIS TREASURE.

God, thank You for the gift of Your word.
As I spend time with You,
the more like You I become.
As I spend time in Your word
and meditate on it the more blessed I am.
Help me to be intentional
about what I meditate on today.
Your word is a lamp to my feet
and a light to my path.

SUCCESS STARTS ON SUNDAY

I was glad when they said to me,
"Let us go to the house of the Lord."

Psalm 122:1

Day 7: Success Starts on Sunday

While it's tough to admit, there was a time in my life when going to church was not something I would look forward to. Those dreaded words "let's go to church" would always make me sad because I did not understand the joy and the power of worshiping God with other faith-filled believers in one place. Several decades later, I am so glad that church is now a part of my life.

When I finally committed to putting God first in my week and discovered that true success in the Kingdom starts on Sunday, it set a tone of joy for my life and for my entire family.

Did you know that there have been a number of scientific studies conducted on the benefits of attending a weekly worship service? It's been proven that people who faithfully commit to worshiping weekly with a community actually live longer, and also believe they have more of a sense of fulfillment and purpose concerning their lives.

And while we appreciate that science shows us living longer lives when we do, we know that as believers, that is not our primary motivation for going to church. We go to church because we are invited to draw near to God. We go to church so we can magnify the Lord together. We go to church because we are commanded not to ever forsake the assembling of ourselves together.

One of the reasons we believe and often say that success begins on Sunday is because over 2,000 years ago, the original founder of the local church, actually walked out of a tomb on a Sunday! Although dead on a Friday, He was made alive on a Sunday!

Every Sunday morning, you and I have been given a weekly opportunity to proclaim throughout the world that Jesus got up and conquered death, hell and the grave.

No matter what we may have faced during the week, Sunday is our chance to come together and lift up the name of Jesus, a name that is above any other name. By coming together every Sunday, we are reminding each other that since His tomb is empty, ours can be as well. This is something we are commanded to do together, because we are simply better when together.

You and I belong in the house of the Lord, and when we commit to doing so each week, we are well on our way to not only leading a God first life, but helping others to do so too.

YOU AND I HAVE BEEN
GIVEN A WEEKLY
OPPORTUNITY
TO PROCLAIM
THROUGHOUT
THE WORLD
THAT JESUS GOT UP AND
CONQUERED DEATH,
HELL AND THE GRAVE.

God, thank You for the gift
of going to church and proclaiming Your goodness.
I commit to giving You my Sundays
and plant myself in Your house, the local church.
Help me to be an active part
and an encouragement to others.
I stand on Your promise
that when I am planted, I will flourish.

BE FRUITFUL

Then God blessed them and said,
"Be fruitful and multiply.
Fill the earth and govern it."

Genesis 1:28

Day 8: Be Fruitful

Have you ever been called lazy before? Not a great feeling, is it? It seems like a harsh word to hear, and perhaps even more harsh to say, but it's a word Jesus actually used when describing those who refused to do something meaningful with the time and talents they were given.

In what is called 'the parable of the talents,' Jesus shares that an owner gave talents to several of his servants before heading off on a journey. When he came back, he discovered that some of the servants reproduced and multiplied what they had, while others chose not to by hiding it. Those that multiplied their talents were given more, but those that did not, he called them lazy. In fact, he not only called them lazy, he called them wicked.

One of the things you and I must understand as believers is how much God has invested into us. When we consider the investment He made using the blood of His very own son, it ought to shape something within our hearts. To knit us together with Him and to provide us with purpose and destiny while we were still in our mother's womb, it ought to spark something within us.

Our God is a God who has invested a lot into us. And He wants a return on His investment.

Everything that God designed was done so with the purpose of being fruitful. Men and women were both created and provided the tools to bring forth life when they come together as one. When we look at nature, specifically how trees and plants reproduce and multiply after themselves, we can see that fruitfulness is something that God expects out of everything that is connected to Him.

When you and I stand before God and hopefully hear those words, "Well done, good and faithful servant," it will most likely be because we followed His Word and were fruitful. God will call us good at the end of our life because we fully embraced what He says about what is right. And He will call us faithful because we weren't satisfied with just showing up in life, but that we were committed to produce a return.

A fruitful harvest of everything He has called us to do.

EVERYTHING THAT GOD DESIGNED WAS DONE SO WITH THE PURPOSE OF BEING FRUITFUL.

God, thank You for giving me gifts and talents.
Thank You for giving me the ability
to use what I have to bring others to You.
I commit to develop me gifts, talents and abilities
so that I can bring sons and daughters
who are far from You into Your family.
I want my life to be full of fruitfulness.

WHAT ARE YOU LOOKING AT?

The eye is the lamp of the body. So then if your eye is clear your whole body will be full of light.

Matthew 6:22

Day 9: What Are You Looking At?

Your vision is a huge determining factor to where you want to go in life. No different than driving a car, we steer in the direction that we stare. In a world full of multiple attractions and distractions whose sole purpose is to pull us away from the things that matter most, what we find ourselves looking at most is very important for us to evaluate as often as we can.

As believers, we should keep our eyes steady on our God, our family, our health and our finances. However, our enemy is well aware of that, and does all he can to break our focus. He knows that when our vision is clear, we are able to see the path God wants us to take. The quality of our life is a direct result of the quality and clarity of our vision.

In order to maintain a God-first life, one that sees clearly and seeks God's kingdom fully, there are a few questions you should ask yourself every day:

Where are you headed? Where do you want to go?
And when you get to where you want to go, where will that be?

No matter which direction we decide to take, we will never end up in the right place if we are not going to the right source for direction. The Holy Spirit is that right source. He is the perfect helper, ready to guide us into all truth when we seek Him with all of our heart. If you are discouraged about where you are today, there's no reason to stay there. God has a great plan and purpose for you, so today, become optimistic and hopeful about where you can go.

Abraham Lincoln once said, "The best way to predict the future is to create it." If you are ready to create a new future, then it's time to begin making some decisions today. Decide what you want out of your life, your marriage, your family, your business and your health. And don't just decide, write it down. Keep your eyes on it.

When you keep your eyes on your vision you are essentially keeping your eyes on your why. And whenever you and I lose our why, we will lose our way. Now is the time to see yourself doing, becoming, and experiencing all that God has destined for your life.

Begin to meditate today quietly before the Lord and watch your vision become a reality. When you acknowledge Him first, you can take confidence that your best days are indeed ahead.

THE QUALITY OF OUR LIFE IS A DIRECT RESULT OF THE QUALITY AND CLARITY OF OUR VISION.

God, thank You for being the author
and finisher of my faith.
Help me to order my life in such a way
that I am partnering with You.
Help me to be fruitful and not scattered.
Help me to hear Your still small voice
guiding and directly my path.
My trust is in You.
The dreams You have placed
in my heart are a gift.
Help to be disciplined and partner
with You and that they may come to pass.

HEALTHY THINGS GROW

Jesus grew in wisdom, stature, and favor with both God and man.

Luke 2:52

It is a common fact and truth that everything that is healthy will grow. This doesn't just apply to natural things around us like plants and animals, but it applies to our lives as well. Our bodies and minds are always growing at the rate of our self-care. The better we treat them, the better we are.

One attribute as believers that we always want to be growing is our wisdom. From the moment we become a child of God, we are on a path of growth, and that growth is strengthened by the wisdom we have in God. What we began as a diet of milk should soon become a one full of solid food. The more we spend time with Christ, the more He is formed inside of us, and the more everything concerning our lives becomes transformed.

It's awesome that Jesus, although equal with God, developed a pattern of growth for us all to follow, where His wisdom and favor grew while here on earth. His wisdom did not just come from within Himself, it came from those He was committed to listen and learn from. The same is true with us. Our journey of growth and wisdom is not only found in the Word of God, but by surrounding ourselves with wise people. In fact, the Bible tells us that we will grow in favor and safety when we have a 'multitude' of counselors. Not just a few, but a multitude.

What wisdom are you in need of today?
Who are you listening to right now that has achieved what you are trying to achieve?

Jesus grew in stature too, not just physically but in his spirit and soul. Jesus learned to recognize opportunities to take action on. He grew in RESPONSE ability - the ability to respond the right way in the right time. God wants us to mature spiritually and grow in responsibility just like Jesus. We are called to grow up in Christ (Eph. 4:15)

Jesus grew in favor by knowing what pleased The Father. God loves us all the same but His favor can grow in our lives as we live with a sincere desire to do what delights him. It is like my children, I love them all deeply and equally but when they desire to do what I have asked them to do especially when they do it without me having to ask them I am inclined to lavish unexpected favor upon them.

The actions you choose to take today can make all the difference in the world. You can become the person of blessing that God wants you to become just by seeking His wisdom every day. When you seek His voice and His values, your wisdom increases in every direction. For those of you who are parents, you know that love and obedience from your children can go a long way. When they are committed to doing what you ask of them, you can't help but to favor them with love and gifts.

Our God is the same way. He loves to provide us with privileges when we begin to show Him that we value what He values, and love what He loves. And when our wisdom grows, we not only grow in our knowledge of Him, our favor with people He wants us to reach and impact will increase as well.

YOU CAN BECOME THE PERSON OF BLESSING THAT GOD WANTS YOU TO BECOME JUST BY SEEKING HIS WISDOM EVERY DAY.

*God, thank You for your wisdom
and for stature and favor with You and
others. Help me to avoid worldly wisdom
and seek Your Word on all matters.
Thank you for sending Godly people into
my life to teach me Your wisdom. Help
me to listen and obey
to the voice of wisdom today.
I know this will mean change
because healthy growth involves change.
Thank You for being with me
through every growing pain.*

ALIGNMENTS & ASSIGNMENTS

*Two people are better off than one,
for they can help each other succeed.*

Ecclesiastes 4:12

It's been said that birds of a feather will flock together. For most of our lives we've been told that our relationships, who we choose to fly through life with, will more often than not determine how high we can reach, and how far we can go. It's true birds of a feather flock together and arrive together, so make sure you know where your flock is headed.

Well the same can apply to how effective we are at leading a God-first life. As believers, who we choose to align ourselves with in life is vital because the purpose and potential God desires us to fulfill is not something we can do alone. Two is always better than one, and God created us to be in a community full of people who are committed to pursuing Him together as the body of Christ.

So how do we determine who we should be connected to and aligned with?

One of the first ways of discovering this is finding people who are moving in the direction we want to go. People with similar values. People who are demonstrating the character of Christ. When we understand that we tend to become the people we are the most intimate with, then taking the time to examine our relationships will be something we will no longer ignore.

It is important to remember that people are like elevators. They can either take us up, or they take us down. And if it seems that you are always down in life, perhaps it's time to change the elevators you've been in. As believers, we have been called to be lifters, always seeking to add value to those in our circle. So if your circle is not adding value to you, be courageous enough to change it today.

When you change your circle, you will change your cycle. Whenever God is ready to do something new in your life, He will often use people to do it. Begin to ask God to send you the right people in your life, and invite Him to also help make you the right person for someone else's life. The best version of you may just be on the other side of a better relationship.

So if success always seems to be out of reach for you, remember that right alignments determine right assignments. If you will begin adjusting your relationships today, it will help establish a better tomorrow.

WHEN YOU CHANGE YOUR CIRCLE, YOU WILL CHANGE YOUR CYCLE.

God, thank You for the gift of Godly relationships.
Help me to develop great relationships
and be a great friend to others.
I thank You for the new people
You are bringing into my life and for removing
wrong relationships from my life as well.
Help me to discern Your alignments for me.

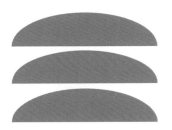

RIGHT THINKING, RIGHT LIVING

As a man thinks in his heart, so is he.

Proverbs 23:7

Day 12: Right Thinking, Right Living

All of us have been guilty at one time or another of having wrong thoughts. They could be wrong thoughts about something, or wrong thoughts about someone. Either way, our way of thinking is often based on how we were raised and what we were taught early on as children. However, as children of God, we have an opportunity to embrace the benefits of a whole new way of thinking.

When you and I align ourselves with the Word of God, we are able to toss aside our old traditions and mindsets and take on those that only reflect the goodness and righteousness of God. We are able to do this because devoting ourselves to the Word of God does not change our mind.

It changes our hearts.

The author of this passage of Proverbs is describing a person who is struggling through life being one way on the outside, and another on the inside. On the outside, he appears to be someone who is generous, but on the inside he is actually a miser, someone who doesn't want to share with anyone. And as we see, he is not putting on this act because of something he thinks in his head. He does so because of the condition of his heart.

Some of us are struggling today in the same way. We often go through life divided between our heart and our mind. When we are not in alignment with what we believe and what we think, it means we aren't living a life that is whole, but one that is fragmented. And when we aren't in the right alignment, everything we try to do will fail.

Friends, God has no interest in us failing. He has called us to prosper! The word prosper means to continuously go forward and upward. If we want to move forward and upward, whether it be in our homes as parents or at our jobs, then we have to begin to exchange our old hearts for His.

When we take the time to truly embrace God's way of thinking, we will never live a divided life, stuck in the old traditions of the past. Whenever we feel stuck in something, it may be an indication that we are believing something that God has not said.

Take confidence today that God's word will never leave you and I stuck. It's sole purpose is to provide us with the right path and the right heart to live a life that is abundant. When we focus our hearts on what He says, will we enter every day with a renewed expectation to prosper!

WHENEVER WE FEEL STUCK IN SOMETHING, IT MAY BE AN INDICATION THAT WE ARE BELIEVING SOMETHING THAT GOD HAS NOT SAID.

God, thank You that You are the way,
the truth and the life.
Create in me a clean and undivided heart
that is committed to walk in Your ways.
I thank You that You desire me
to prosper and I stand on Your promises.

BE FRUITFUL AGAIN

When you produce much fruit,
you are my true disciples.
This brings great glory to my Father.

John 15:8

We love to describe our God as a God of increase because He saw fit to give His creation the ability to grow, to reproduce and to multiply. Although there are some who struggle with the idea that God is highly interested in growth, when you take time to study nature and how it behaves, you can clearly see that increase is indeed the heart of God.

We've said it before but it bears repeating: our God wants us to be fruitful.

Whether it is in our marriages, our families or our finances, God wants us to increase in every area of our life. He wants us to increase in our purpose. To increase in our love and generosity to others. He also wants us to increase in our relationship with Him, which comes with increasing our knowledge of His Word. In order for His kingdom to expand throughout the earth, it requires for us to maintain a faithful commitment to grow and to increase.

Earlier on in this passage of scripture, Jesus describes Himself as a vine, and those of us who believe in Him as His branches. If you have ever seen a fruit vine in person, you know that the branches are only alive and productive when they are connected to the vine. As His branches, the same is true with us. When we are committed to staying connected to God through His Word and through prayer, we are essentially staying connected to a source of constant increase for our lives.

When we agree to abide in His presence, we rarely have to worry about the results. God does that for us. There's nothing we have to do or make happen. When we abide in Him, fruit happens. By producing fruit, we are demonstrating the difference between simply being a believer and being a disciple. A disciple is someone who doesn't just believe in God, he or she is connected to God.

Connection always produces, and when we are connected to the right things, it can produce a life of joy. Did you realize the most fulfilled and happiest people on the planet are those people who are being productive? They're not just being busy doing things that don't matter, but they're being fruitful because they are focused only on what will bring results.

Perhaps today is one that you just aren't experiencing the results you are looking for. It could be a season of barrenness or one that feels like a dry wilderness. Well, we've got good news for you. Where you are now is not where you have to stay. Just like a branch connected to a vine, there are seasons where God desires for us to be pruned. It's not that He is mad at us, but so He can produce more fruit in and through us.

More often than not, God wants us to grow there before we go there. This season of focus and discipline can produce an amazing harvest of fruit if you lean into God's presence. Believe today that where you are is designed for increase. This pruning has a purpose.

Once you realize that you were created to multiply and produce, you will begin to see that what God has for you just ahead may in fact be your best season yet.

GOD WANTS US TO GROW THERE BEFORE WE GO THERE.

God, thank You for giving me the ability
to grow in every area of my life.
Help me to love Your training and discipline.
Thank You for the gift of abiding
in You for I know when I am connected to You,
my life will overflow with fruitfulness.
I don't have to strive.
I just need to abide.

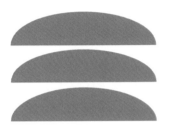

MAKE THE COMMITMENT

And may you be completely faithful
to the Lord our God.
May you always obey his decrees and commands,
just as you are doing today.

1 Kings 8:61

It's been said that motivation is what may get you started, but commitment is what will keep you going. Despite that truth, it is amazing how many people are actually afraid of making commitments, especially long-term ones. It can make some feel trapped, but the truth is, in order for us to truly be successful in life, we have to be willing to make some commitments.

Whether it is a commitment to ourselves, to others, or to God, it takes great intentionality whenever we are choosing to pursue new paths and outcomes for our lives. But we can take assurance that God is with us and for us, ready to guide and ready to support us.

Making new decisions can always be difficult, especially when it comes to our health, wealth or relationships. We often struggle with the idea of giving up something to get something, but it is in our willingness to give up what no longer is sustaining us that God begins to help us build up the character and integrity we need for the future.

As believers, God requires us to be accountable for every commitment we make. And accountability to God looks a lot like being all in, holding nothing back at all. Our love for Him is predicated on that one word: all. To give Him all of our heart, all of our soul, and all of our mind leaves no room for doubt. He requires our full commitment and He expects us to always be people whose word is firm and unwavering.

When you say you're going to do something, then you do it. No matter how tough the circumstances, you refuse to quit. I'm sure we all have encountered people who were just on the verge of a major breakthrough, but decided to quit instead. How many marriages could have made it if they had just decided to go to counseling instead of the courtroom? How much different would our bodies look today if we had decided to continue to eat differently and exercise more consistently, instead of throwing in the towel after just a few weeks?

No matter what area in our lives requires more commitment from us to change, we have to be willing to stay the course. One area that we all could use a lot more commitment is in the reading of God's Word. For it is in His Word, where we are can be stirred up daily to pursue His best for our life. In fact, it is amazing that the more you read His Word, the more you will want to read it. The same is true with prayer and with worship. The more you do it, the more you will want to do it. Our motivation for commitment grows whenever we refuse to quit.

Today, let's take on that attitude, an attitude that is ready to pursue God's best no matter the cost. When we are committed to go all in, we will never fail in the sight of God.

OUR MOTIVATION FOR COMMITMENT GROWS WHENEVER WE REFUSE TO QUIT.

God, thank You for Your commitment to me.
May I be fully committed to being my best for You.
Help me to be steadfast and to never give up.
Thank You that when I fall,
You are there to help me back up.
I refuse to go backward or to stop.
I know others are counting on me
and with You on my side I will not fail.

A HEART
OF GENEROSITY

For wherever your treasure is,
there your heart will be also.

Matthew 6:21

Day 15: A Heart of Generosity

If you want to know what the key is to having a more intimate relationship with God, it is found in one simple word: generosity. Giving is the gateway to more intimacy with God, because we are never more like God than we are generous with what is most important to us.

Jesus makes it clear in this passage that our heart can not be separated from our treasure. In fact, our treasure never follows our heart, it is our heart that follows our treasure. What we value most can be seen when we examine our finances, as well as what we value least. As believers, we want to commit ourselves to a life of generosity, a life where His Kingdom is first concerning our money.

If we want our heart to remain close to God, then our treasure must be put in Him and what He loves. And what He loves more than anything is His kingdom. It should be a joy and an honor for us to give towards Kingdom work whenever we can. Giving should never be a burden or something that grieves us. We never have to worry about sacrificing our finances for His Kingdom because our God is someone we can never out give. He will never owe us. And we give beyond our comfort levels, we are able to access and experience His presence in ways unimaginable.

Our giving is the purest form of worship that we have. We are drawn closer to God every time we do.

It is important to understand that God does not need our money or our treasure. It is our heart that He's after. He is well aware that gaining wealth outside of Him will not fulfill us. We are only fulfilled when we become a vehicle through which God can give to others. When our families, neighbors and strangers can experience God through our giving, we are able to see what a true treasure really looks like.

Our God gives us the free will to do what we want with our treasure, and as believers, we should choose Him over all. His kingdom and His righteousness is what we seek. It is what living and leading a God-first life is all about.

If you are determined to leave a legacy in the earth, and to make sure what you're doing today will be remembered by your children's children, then begin to live a life of generosity. Don't allow fear to stop you from becoming a giver. Always remember that whenever you give, people will get saved, you and I get blessed, but God will get the glory.

God is ready and willing to multiply whatever you give to Him when you do so in faith and with your whole heart.

OUR GIVING IS THE PUREST FORM OF WORSHIP THAT WE HAVE.

*God, thank You for giving Your one
and only Son in exchange for my life.
You are the ultimate giver.
Let my life be a constant act of worship
as I give it to You.
I give You my heart, my time,
my resource and all my abilities
to use for Your purpose.
Keep me from selfish desires
and help me to live a life marked by generosity.*

WORDS, DEEDS AND SEEDS

Do not be deceived.
God is not mocked.
For whatever one sows,
that he will also reap.

Galatians 6:7

A   AG

Day 16: Words, Deeds and Seeds

There is a principle and process of growth that God placed into existence before you and I were ever born and it is what He calls seed-time and harvest. This principle points to the fact that whatever you and I choose to do today will produce results tomorrow, whether they be good or bad. Every single day, no matter what we may believe we are in lack of, we have the opportunity to plant and sow the seeds that we believe we will produce and reap a great harvest.

One of the most potent and powerful seeds God has given us to sow into the world is our words. Every word we say is a seed, and they have the potential to build others up and to tear them down based upon the level of love, honesty and grace in which we say them. The same is true with our deeds, the things we actually do in life. Every deed we do is a seed, and if we choose to do good and uphold the righteousness of God with our thoughts and actions, we are able to harvest good for ourselves in return.

God makes it crystal clear for us here in Galatians that there is no way around the process of reaping. Everything we give will be returned to us eventually. By the measure we give it, we will receive it back. That's why sowing as much as we possibly can is so very important if we want our futures to look different. But the truth is, one of the biggest reasons we don't sow is because we want our reaping season and harvest to happen quickly.

When we think in more natural terms, sowing can take time. When you plant fruit or vegetable seeds, you don't see an immediate return once that seed hits the ground. It takes time and a great deal of patience. But when the harvest comes, it is far greater than the seed we first planted. An apple tree doesn't just produce one apple, but baskets full of apples season after season, year after year. The same is true when we sow spiritually.

The little we sow every day, we can be sure that God is able and willing to do much with it. Let's sow some seeds of faith today, in both word and deed. No matter where you may be or what you may believe you don't have, take confidence that you will reap a great harvest.

ONE OF THE MOST POTENT AND POWERFUL SEEDS GOD HAS GIVEN US TO SOW INTO THE WORLD IS OUR WORDS.

*God, thank You for blessing me
with Your loving words.
As I reflect on what Your Word says about me.
I see clearly the power of words.
Help me to be generous with my words,
sowing life into the lives of those around me.
Help me to be patient in the process
for I know I will see Your Word
come to pass in your time.*

REDEEM THE TIME

Make the most of every opportunity because the days are evil.

Ephesians 5:16

Day 17: Redeem the Time

The Bible tells us that when we compare the length of our life to that of eternity, it is just a vapor. It's short and flies by us no matter how much we pray for it to slow down. We can't make more of it, and unfortunately, tend to waste more than actually invest.

When it comes to the concept of time, the Apostle Paul says that it is very important for us to redeem it as much as possible. Not spend it or waste it, but redeem it. The word redeem literally means to put time back where it belongs. It means to prioritize our time knowing that our days here on earth are numbered and as Paul describes: evil. Time is not something we should ever believe we have an abundance of. God is very clear that we should make every day count as though it is our very last.

It's important to know that what you and I order in life will determine our capacity. More often than not, the order of our day begins with a ton of distractions. Studies show that we are distracted almost every three minutes, which is why we tend to look back at our days and wonder what in the world did we do with our time. Our minds are wired for distraction, which is why it is so vital to begin each day giving God the first order and place of our time. When we make time with Him our highest core value, He provides us the wisdom to steward our time, and to make a greater impact with it.

Setting a new precedent with our time and how we can maximize it better by putting God first protects us from waste. In fact, it helps us stop over-estimating the time we have tomorrow, and helps us under-estimate and appreciate what we have available to us today. Once you embrace the simple fact that eternity is forever, heaven is real and hell is hot, the idea of redeeming the time becomes so much easier.

Let's make God's kingdom today a renewed focus for our life. Let's have a sense of urgency about putting His values first, and less of an urgency about things that really aren't that important. What should be important today is our time in worship, our time in prayer, our time spent with our family, and our time serving a world that is desperately in need of hope.

Let's agree to no longer put off what needs to get done today. Let's begin redeeming our time and watch how God increases our productivity in every area of our lives.

TIME IS NOT SOMETHING WE SHOULD EVER BELIEVE WE HAVE AN ABUNDANCE OF.

God, thank You for the gift of time.
Forgive me for the time I have wasted.
Help me to redeem the number of days
and live a life that pleases You.
A life dedicated to making
the most of every opportunity.
Help me to see the urgency of the mission.
I devote myself today to obedience
and to being led by Your spirit.

GIVING LOVES COMPANY

Let us think of ways to motivate
one another to acts of love and good works.
And let us not neglect our meeting together,
as some people do, but encourage one another,
especially now that the day of His return is drawing near.

Hebrews 10:24-25

Day 18: Giving Loves Company

As believers, there is something special and supernatural that happens whenever we come together. Whether it is for the purpose of worshiping on Sunday or connecting during the week to build healthy relationships with each other. However, one moment that seems to top them all is when we come together for the purpose of giving and serving.

There is something about generosity and actually seeing others give away what is important to them that inspires others to grow. As the body of Christ, a body that has been created to fit and function together with purpose, when we choose to love others by giving away our time, talent and treasure, we are able to demonstrate the primary purpose God has us here on earth.

While giving is fun to do alone, it is so much better when we do it alongside others. Giving in isolation often is about our own self-gratification, but when we give openly and as a group or family, the world can't help but to stand back and take notice.

Our God was such a great example of this kind of public generosity, as the book of Genesis tells us He saw fit to consult with His own personal company in the person of Jesus and the Holy Spirit when creating us. His generosity continued thousands of years later, when giving up His own son to die and take on the penalty for our sin. That gift was not a private one, but a public one; a gift that has redeemed our lives for eternity.

What public act of generosity can you display today? Who is in need of your time, your listening ear, or perhaps even some of your finances? What other people at your job or your church can you connect with this week and together bless someone when they least expect it.

As believers, we should never be in lack to give because God's Word tells us that the generous soul will always prosper. God has made it so that your current generosity and your future prosperity are inseparable. So if you seem to be prospering less today, try giving more.

You'll be glad you did.

GOD HAS MADE IT
SO THAT YOUR
CURRENT
GENEROSITY AND
YOUR FUTURE
PROSPERITY ARE
INSEPARABLE.

A God-First Life

*God, thank You for the single greatest act
of generosity - the cross.
Thank You that when I give along
with my brothers and sisters in Christ,
that we are giving as one body.
I thank You that our generosity
is multiplied and the momentum is unstoppable.
Help me to continue a life
of generosity until the whole world hears
Your beautiful gospel.*

KEEP PLANTING

Remember this, a farmer who plants only a few seeds will get a small crop, but the one who plants generously will get a generous crop.

2 Corinthians 9:6

Day 19: Keep Planting

While most of us did not have the opportunity to grow up on a farm, you would have thought that the Apostle Paul may have. Through many of the letters in the New Testament, he loved to provide life lessons that had to do with planting crops. Especially when conveying the importance of giving our best to God.

When writing to a church in Corinth, Paul shared a blueprint of how our financial giving can be compared to planting seeds. In essence, the seeds we sow have been created by God to reproduce what is inside of it. If we plant orange seeds, we should reproduce orange trees. If we plant lemon or apple seeds, lemon and apple trees are what we will reproduce. No matter how hard we pray for a different kind of fruit to appear, we receive based on the seeds we sow.

Paul also shares that our giving is not just based on what we sow. The more we sow, the more we are able to receive. And the less we sow, the smaller our return. However, what's great about God's system of sowing and reaping is that when we give generously, He does as well.

Whenever we give, He is faithful to multiply it. When we give to His Kingdom and to the local church, when we give to those in need, and to do with a cheerful and joyful heart, we are essentially releasing seed as a sower into a ground that will always reproduce greater than what we gave. In fact, when it comes to sowing seed and giving God your very best, here is something you should try saying whenever what you have appears to be too small:

"What's in my hand is the most it will ever be. But when I give this, when it leaves my hand, it's the least it will ever be."

Repeating that simple phrase every time to yourself can help shift you from simply wanting to be blessed, to becoming a blessing for others. When we give generously, our needs will always be taken care of, and best of all, God's kingdom is expanded.

You and I rarely see or have heard of a farmer complaining about a harvest that hasn't come in yet. He doesn't get weary and he doesn't quit, because He understands what due season is all about. The same needs to be true for us. When we sow our best, and have not seen a return yet, there's no need for discouragement. We simply need to keep sowing.

Your due season will come. Keep sowing, growing and giving. And watch for a harvest that is far beyond what was in your hand.

WHAT'S IN MY HAND IS
THE MOST IT
WILL EVER BE.
BUT WHEN I GIVE THIS,
WHEN IT LEAVES
MY HAND,
IT'S THE LEAST
IT WILL EVER BE.

God, thank You that your ways
are right and good.
They often seem opposite
to the world's way of doing things.
When I give, You said I will receive
something greater.
It's a divine exchange.
Keep my heart pure
and generous before You.
Help me to live with an open hand.
I know I could never outgive You,
but help me to desire to give more.
I want to continually grow in generosity.

A TREASURED WITNESS

Therefore, go and make disciples of all the nations,
baptizing them in the name of the Father
and the Son and the Holy Spirit.
Teach these new disciples to obey
all the commands I have given you.
And be sure of this:
I am with you always, even to the end of the age.

Matthew 28:19-20

Day 20: A Treasured Witness

If you love old pirate tales or movies, you know all about how they love to find hidden treasure. Pirates search all over for treasure chests that may have fallen to the bottom of the ocean from some long lost ship or wreck. Those chests would often be filled to the brim with rubies and diamonds, making whatever pirate was fortunate enough to find it wealthy beyond his dreams. Well, the greatest treasure you and I can ever find is not hidden inside a chest.

It is hidden inside the good news of Jesus Christ. There is nothing that can outweigh the value of receiving the good news of who Jesus Christ is, but sharing it with others - that is priceless.

You and I share good news about something every day. It could be a product we love or a recent movie we've seen. But when we share the good news of Jesus, and the grace He so generously has given to us, the reward is so much greater than anything else in the world.

In fact, this passage in Matthew is what we call the 'Great Commission' - it was one of the last things Christ asked His disciples to do before ascending to Heaven. While most of us believe this command to us to share the good news looks like a fancy sermon or perfected monologue, it is actually just generosity in action. Simple acts of generosity that we can share every day.

Is there anything God has done for you? Share it. Is there anything God has said to you? Share it. How different has your life been since you've turned it over to God? Share it.

The commission is all about sharing and being a witness for someone. It's about being open with your life and always looking for someone who is in need of the goodness of God. Is there someone you know that needs more of God? Why not try sharing more of you?

The more you and I become a witness for God, the more opportunities He provides for us to be one. He loves to trust us with more people to bless when we have proven faithful to share what we ourselves have been blessed with. There is no greater act of generosity than sharing the treasure we have found in God.

It literally can turn a life of piracy into a life of eternal blessing. And that's a life worth living.

THERE IS NO GREATER
ACT OF GENEROSITY
THAN SHARING
THE TREASURE
WE HAVE FOUND
IN GOD.

*God, thank You for sending
someone to tell me
about the treasure of Your goodness.
Help me to be bold in sharing You with others.
Send people across
my path today that need You.
Help to be me aware
of how I can share the treasure
of Your love with them.*

OUR GREATEST TOOL

Tell them to use their money to do good.
They should be rich in good works
and generous of those in need,
always being ready to share with others.
By doing this they will be storing up
their treasure as a good foundation
for the future, so they may experience true life.

1 Timothy 6:18-19

Day 21: Our Greatest Tool

This final devotion is one we believe will provide you with one of the most important philosophies we as believers need to have in order to be successful in living and leading a God-first life, especially when it comes to our money. Once this philosophy is fully embraced, you will never have a problem receiving money, managing money, and most importantly, being a blessing to others with your money.

So here it is: our money is a tool.

This tool is one given to us by God as a gift to unlock everything we believe we are in lack of concerning our lives. When we see money as a tool and a gift, we no longer place our focus on possessions and experiences in this life that have no heavenly good. We no longer are consumed with earthly things, because our treasure is no longer found in money. It is found in how we can use money to store up greater treasures; the kind that will last beyond us.

Many of us understand (or should understand) the importance of saving and spending money wisely. There is wisdom in having good things in life, but not letting things have us. When we spend wisely, we place less stock in what is temporary and have room for what is eternal. But God wants us to be much more than wise spenders and savers of our money.

He wants us to be extravagant givers of our money too.

The Apostle Paul shares in this passage that we have not experienced true life until we have become generous givers. When we live with an eternal perspective concerning our money, how when invested into God's kingdom, our money can actually make us rich in good works, that is when this tool of generosity is used the way God designed it.

As believers, when we give our treasure on Earth we are making an eternal difference in the lives of people and we are storing up treasure in heaven. We can't take our treasure with us but can deposit it into our eternal future. Jesus commanded us to do so, when He said don't store up treasures on Earth but rather in heaven where they will last for us forever. We ought to get excited about treasures that will last for an eternity. If heaven is our goal, then how we spend our money here on earth should reflect that. Today, why don't you try challenging yourself to become a generous giver.

No matter what you've given in the past, there is still an opportunity to stretch and invest more into those around you and to what God loves more than anything, the ministry of the local church. We have the greatest tool to make a lasting difference in the earth.

So let's use it together. Today.

IF HEAVEN IS OUR GOAL, THEN HOW WE SPEND OUR MONEY HERE ON EARTH SHOULD REFLECT THAT.

CONCLUSION

Leading a God first life is simply deciding to put God first in everything and then manage that decision daily. When we focus on doing what matters most we will live a life that most matters. When we restore the order of doing things God's way we will see Him add all things that matter to our lives both here and in eternity. You can lead the God first life, one step at a time, one foot in front of the other. When you do what's necessary to win the day you will see God's divine momentum move you forward. Let's go!

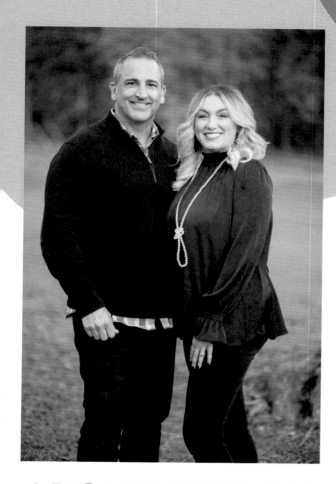

ABOUT THE AUTHORS

Pastors Michael & Charla Turner are the founding pastors of Turning Point Church, a multi-site, multi-cultural and multi-generational church located throughout South Atlanta, Georgia. With a passion to see the fatherless restored, to help people identify their gifts and lead a God-first life, Michael and Charla are the proud parents of three children. For more information about them and Turning Point Church, you can log onto TurningPoint.Church.